Are You Hurting Too?

What the silence left behind

ANAHA

Tinted Mirrorball

First published by Tinted Mirrorball 2025 Copyright ©

To my wonderful grandparents
Mandya Ajji and Tha

You will always and forever mean the world to me.

In the end
you became another story
I never wanted to write-
But I wrote anyway.

A question echoing
in the back of my mind-
'*Are You Hurting Too?*'

-APRIL

Contents

Preface

This book isn't about me. It's about *you.*

This book is split into four parts:

1. **What Darkness Spoke** – The pain we tend to hide. Big and small.
2. **I Loved** – The soft parts of us, the parts that still believes in love. Love that comes in all shapes and forms.
3. **I Let Go** – The strength and the weakness we find when we have to walk away.
4. **I Let Life Speak** – The different ways my eyes saw the world. The secrets and the obvious.

These poems are yours now, to hold when it gets too heavy.
Take what you need and leave the rest.
But just know- you are not alone.

Acknowledgments

I want to thank my mum, my dad, my aunts, my uncle, and most of all, my grandparents, for all their support and encouragement. I also want to thank all my amazing friends for their love, support, and for simply being there- giving me suggestions, offering kind words, and cheering me on throughout.

A special thanks to my Mumziee and to my best friend, Arvind, who have always taken out time from their busy schedules to check each and every poem, each and every word- helping me with everything from tips on how I can improve to helping me navigate Word Document.

Mumziee, thank you so much for always supporting me and being my rock- even when I doubted myself or was going through complications. More than anything, thank you for being someone I know I can trust to help me fix anything I'm struggling with or need help on.

I wouldn't have been able to do it without all of you.
I have truly been blessed. Thank you, and love you all.

I

WHAT DARKNESS SPOKE

Like a cracker,
I burst into the most spectacular sparkle—
A show worth watching
A show as mesmerizing as life itself.

But what nobody noticed was,
I burst into *pieces*—
Sparkling,
Yet *burning*.

That—
It tore me apart,
It shredded me to bits.
I was all over the place.

I shattered in the most spectacular fashion—
But shatter, I did.

I looked in the mirror,
And my mask fell off.
As I repeatedly chanted,
"*You deserved better.*"

As though comforting another,
Because that's all I've ever known,
Comforting another—
This girl in the mirror.

I'm a single candle
Flickering in the dark,
Fighting against the *gushing wind*
That is trying to blow me apart,
That is threatening to extinguish me,
As if to *silence me.*

Grasping onto dear life —
For if I let go,
I know there is no coming back.

This light, ever so faint,
I fight for,
With darkness
Trying to devour my heart.

A matter of time
Is all I've got
Before this candle in me
Goes *forever dark.*

My heart begged,
"*Cut your hair*"
But my mind knew the pain—
The pain of cutting my hair.

So, I sat there,
Cutting myself
Limb by limb,
Till I bled
All throughout the room

-The room that houses my soul.

Maybe 'cause somewhere deep within,
I know I'm just a ticking time bomb—
A bomb that's not only going to end me,
But disrupt everything around me.

Maybe that's why,
Hating myself comes easier
Than hating those
Who have wronged me.

Cause I spent all my life
Loving you —
You,
Who has wronged me
Every step of the way.

Easier,
Since I've been taught
To hate myself
All my life.

I keep letting heavy hearts
rest on me.
Now I am *crumbling*
With the weight I bare—
Unable to carry,
Unable to let go.

Yet,
I never say no,
For who knows
What weight others must carry.

Cuts on my wrists,
As blood slowly drips
Down my fingers.
Red,
like dangling rubies.

My eyes,
Flooded with tears,
Glaring at my cat,
Who sits alone
In a corner,
Licking her *claws*.

Although in pain,
I look down
At my now scarlet hand,
Admiring it—

-My cat's work of art.

I chopped off my hair
Because hair holds memories,
And I wanted no memories
Left of you.

How stupid.
The only thing I ended up losing
Was my hair.
While all the memories still burning
Deep into my skin.

The smell of burning flesh
Up my nose,
Gushing through my body
Every time I inhale.

To the yellow lilies I grew on
my terrace—
Where are you now?
I loved you so much
That I spread your seeds
onto every pot
I could possibly find,
Till you became an infestation.

Just the way I do with love—
Spreading them
All around
Within me,
Till they become an infestation
I can't seem to escape from.

So when they vanish,
Like how you did—
My yellow lilies,
I'm left to feel the rotting roots
rotting within me
Decaying—
Where love once grew.

Touching my guitar
Brings back memories.

For a split second,
It reminds me of who I was—
And I embody her.
That girl,
Who will forever have my heart.

As I hold it,
I feel everything.
Everything—
I felt back then.

So I just sit there
In utter silence,
Hugging my guitar,
Breathing deep—
Trying to comfort that girl,
Who needed
And deserved
All the comforting she could get.

Comforting me.

II

I LOVED

Why does my heart
Ask me to let go,
When my mind
Whispers 'Stay'?

Why does my mind
Ask me to let go,
When my heart
Begs me to stay?

I found me a special someone
Someone as dark and wounded as I.

Dark and wounded were we,
With pain and agony,
Sitting in our clouds of
Demons and misery.

Sharing our darkness,
We ignite—
Like the sun himself,
We alight.
Our clouds together
Cause sparks,
Like thundering light.

Creating art on the canvas
We call the sky,
Magnificently,
Yet,
So full of plight.

We both know the game by now.
This game we have been at for months.

You call me a pain;
With a smirk on your face,
Like you mean it,
but really, you just enjoy it.

I roll my eyes, laughing,
While acting annoyed.

Making fun of each other—
Never too deep,
Never too real.

A friendship laced with something.
Something that is just this.
Something that is just us.

You make plans,
And I always show,
Always just a little late.

I say I hate you,

Which makes you grin,
Like you win.

But in this game,
Where the margins are *thin*,
Will we break free?
Or stay forever—
Locked in.

I started writing you a letter,
Almost telling you—
I never want to lose you.

Almost telling you—
How vulnerable I am with you.

Almost telling you—
The toll your absence takes on me.

Almost—
A mistake.

I told myself I'd moved on,
So why did I go back to square one
When he sent me a picture of your profile?

Why did I click the message,
'Look who popped up on my feed'?

My body reacting
Before my mind ever could.

My body,
That somehow listens to you
Even when it's mine to own.

Because I knew
He was talking about *you*.

Why do I still dream of bumping into you?
Why do I know the exact stories I'd tell you—
Stories you missed out on,
Stories I wish you knew?

Why do I, somewhere deep within,
Still wish your name pops up on my phone,
On a warm sunny afternoon,

When I'm lazing around in bed?

Even when I have not a clue
As to what to say—
or do.

If I close my eyes,
I can still hear
Your *sweet, sweet* voice
Calling my name.

As *"Annu"* echoes through the air,
Within the cold, empty walls I've built,
Trapping the warm memories
of yesterday.

Yes,
I hated you.
Then why do your memories linger
Like a warm embrace,
On a freezing day—
In a *cold, heartless* December?

I almost texted you today.
It felt like the right thing to do.
Then why did my fingers refuse to move?

They refused to type.
The more I pushed forward,
The more they fought back.

So I sat there,
Waiting—
Hoping they'd change their mind.

Staring—
At the blinking cursor
That sat there patiently,
Waiting in anticipation.

Minutes felt like hours.
And the hollowness in my chest
Just kept growing.

Until I embodied a black hole—
Sucking in light,
Drowning in darkness.

I hate you,
'Cause I can't stop loving you.

I want to cut all ties with you,
'Cause they are all tied—
Tugging at my heart.

You,
Wrapped around by my heartstrings.

But chopping them would mean—
Blood
Spilling,
Splashing,
Dripping,
Onto the white marble floor.

So what should I choose?
What will I choose?

Almost dying from pain once and for all,
Or
Hurting a bit, uncontrollably, constantly?

And just like that
We went back to square one

Me,
Asking ChatGPT
To find ways,
Reasons,
Excuses
To meet you.

Just like I had done
At the very beginning.

Isn't the entire point of life
To take chances—
On dreams that seem crazy?

Crazy,
To those around
But feel like destiny to us?

Maybe that's why I chose you.
Because you felt like destiny
To me.

I was in love,
Not with *you.*
But with the way
You loved *me.*

The attention
You gave me.
How my slightest
Actions and movements
Caused tsunamis within you.

I loved everything—
Everything…
Except for *you.*

-Do I call it love?

III

I LET GO

I knew it would kill me to leave you,
So I cut all ties
I had knotted with you.

I told you,
"Decide.
If you're all in
Or—
Just here till our next fight."

While I had my bags packed
All along,
From the very beginning.

Scared to fall,
But falling
All along.

You—
So *right*
Yet couldn't be more wrong.
Wrong—
For me.

And I loved you
More than anything else
In this world.

I loved you
Till your ego was swollen.
Until you thought
You were the one with the magic —
The magic of being lovable.

So you left
And tried to take my love with you,
But soon realized
It wasn't you;
It was me.

I was the one with the magic,
The magic—
That was showered on you
Till you were drenched with ego.

But in a flash,
The world humbled you;
And you came back

Begging me
For my magical love.

Only this time,
I felt no love,
No hate,
No pain,
No anger.

-Just felt the cold feeling of nothingness.

Today I stumbled across a picture of you
and my heart skipped a beat.

It was completely distorted and blurry —
Something I would struggle to figure out
as to who it was.

But that's how I knew,
Just how well
I knew you
Inside and out.

That within a millisecond
Of my eyes landing on it
I knew it was you.

When I really wished
I didn't.

When I finally saw your notification pop up,
After all those months,
I felt the smile on my face
Wash away —
Leaving nothing but *bitterness*
in its wake.

Strange —
How a few months ago,
Your texts used to light up my world,
But now
All it did was darken it
With *disgust*.

If I got a chance to destroy you,
Would I?

Would I spill the lies
you wove around me?

Would I tell the world
all that you did to me?

Would I tell them
all that you didn't?

Would I—

You gave up on us,
So tell me —
How does it feel?
Now that I've finally given up on you.

You,
Back, *begging* for crumbs
Of my belief and affection.

Belief that you could ever be anything
Other than the horrible person
You have always been.

I look at you,
And the world fractures.
Every cruel action,
Every calculated wound,
Replays in my mind,
As I reel with *contempt.*

You stand there smiling
Like a pure, virtuous *saint.*
As though
Redeemed from all wrongs.

While I,
A storm,
Raging silently—

Trees trembling,
As I uproot them with my fury,
Their roots tearing free from the earth,
Like my composure,
Rising with rage and fury.

I call upon the skies—
Thunder roars,
Lightning strikes,

Setting the uprooted trees ablaze.

As flames dance around the sky,
Mimicking the wrath
Dancing within me,
Spiraling upwards,
Craving destruction—
Like my anger, consuming the air.

I stand in its center,
A *witch* being burnt in her skin.

The fire slowly fades,
And the trees root themselves back into the earth.
I catch my breath,
Grasping onto composure
That is trying to slip between my fingers—
Right away.

The trees stand still,
The sky remains calm.
I have destroyed nothing,
Yet I'm covered in ashes
On the *inside*—
Destroying everything within.

The last bouquet of flowers you gave me,
Sat untouched.

I reached for them
And held the weathering flowers
in my soft, warm hands.

Admiring them with love,
Touching them so gently.
The walls watched—
Green with *envy*.

I took a deep breath in
And tossed them in the bin.
Without a second glance,
I turned and walked away,
Just the way you had done
All those months ago.

The walls *cracking*—
Mimicking that of a broken heart
As they stare at the withered flowers
Where, for months they now sat,
Claiming the bin as their own,
Making the bin their new home.

While I tell myself each day—

"*Tomorrow,*
I will finally let them go"

I reached for your hand,
Hoping it would protect me.
But you were *Scar*—
And I,

Mufasa.

I thought we had made peace with our past
And somewhere, I was right.

I made peace with it—
I *moved on.*

While you,
Made peace with it—
But…

We got close—
A bit too close

Close enough to fight over blood and pain,
And all the things
I wished you would—
But you never could
Understand.

So I left,
Walking away
With my pride
Hanging by a thread.

But now,
Here I sit
Half wishing—
I could undo it,
Half knowing—
I never should.

You walked away,
But I wish you nothing but the best.

I wish you all the happiness,
All the success,
But most of all—
A whole lot of *character development.*

So if we ever meet again,
I can smile,
Knowing my prayers came true,
Knowing you're happy,
Knowing you got everything—
Everything you ever wanted.

I hope you smile too;
So I'll know you missed me.
So we'll know—
We missed each other.

This is me
Saying goodbye.

As you hang on the tip—
The tip of my heart,
Slipping—
slowly
But—
A little *too fast*.
Too fast for me.

As I try to pull you back in,
Into my heart.
Trying to stop what's left of you
From slipping out.

Efforts, all in vain.

Having to say goodbye—
For my feelings for you
Refuse to stay put
Within the four walls
Of my so-called heart

You're going to realize
Everything you had
When you had me.

And on that day
You will feel like you were hit—
Hit by a train.

It'll all dawn on you;
All that you had,
And all that you lost.

And that will be the last day
You will ever truly know peace.

Because from that day forward,
You will be hunted.
Haunted—
By everything you did to lose me,
And everything you did after.

Instead of coming back,
Pleading—
On your knees,

Begging me
To take you back.

And on that day,
I pray
The Universe goes easy on you,
Being merciful.

For your sake.

Your name, that used to stand out
Everywhere in my mind,
And on every corner of my eye,
Has now just become a part of the crowd.

Your Display Picture used to be all my eyes found —
And if they couldn't,
It used to be all they searched for.
The slightest glimpse,
They would catch it.

But today?
My eyes don't seem to register it,
Although I scroll right through,
Passing it by.

My eyes don't register it —
Even though I'm looking right at you.
Your picture has just become a picture,
Your name has just become a name.

Although I can swear —
It wasn't at all the same
Till yesterday…

And so I stopped trying
To hold onto you,
To fix things,
To mend us.

And most of all —
T*rying.*

After all, it would only last a week.
For I know you,
I know me,
I know us.

It won't be long
Before we end up
In this same spot again,
For the millionth time

Me, again,
The only one trying
To fix things,
To mend things,
To hold on —
Trying
While you?

-Nothing but a manchild.

I feel nothing when I think of you
Then why does it leave a bad taste in my mouth?

IV

I LET LIFE SPEAK

The sun through the window
Turned the room *juicy orange.*
So heavenly.

But the only admirers?
The memories—
Clinging onto the peeling paint.

Terrified to let go,
Yet they cling onto peeling paint,
Paint that will let go
Falling
Any minute,
Any day.

Frightened to be forgotten,
Forgotten forever—
By the one who remembers.

So scared of abandonment,
Even after being abandoned,
Clinging onto false hope—

A figment of imagination,
As reality becomes insufferable.

Afraid to be forgotten,

Afraid to be replaced,
Afraid to be abandoned,
By the creator of the memories.

Unable to accept the new reality—
A reality, more old than new.
Unable to accept it's over.

For at the end,
Aren't we all just memories
Clinging onto peeling paint?

Maybe all the cruel things you did to me,
Was the Universe
Trying to protect me.

Making sure you did all that you did,
So I'd walk away —
Never looking at you the same.

How many versions of us
Are we mourning
In silence?

The dreams
We left behind,
The actions
We didn't take…

Tell me,
How many versions of us
Are we mourning
In silence?

The decisions
We took,
The moves
We made…

Tell me,
How many versions of us
Are we mourning
In silence?

What if you took a chance right now?
What if you followed your dreams?

Just tell me —
How many **less** versions of you
Will you be mourning
In silence?

There—
In my hands
In black and white
Sat my will.

My will?
I sat there wondering.
At the end,
Is it truly my will?

Does *this will* have anything to do with *my will*?

'Maybe in another life,
Maybe in another reality.'

We keep saying it.
We keep praying for it.

But what if—
This is that life?
This is that reality?

The one we begged for,
The one we cried for,
In a time we can't remember.

What if—
We were given our chance in this life
And like fools
We tossed it away,
Saying—

'Maybe in another life.
Maybe in another reality.'

Paint me pink,
Paint me dark,
Paint me maroon.

And if that doesn't do it—

Color me deep,
Color me dark,
Color me tragically black.

I try to write it all down
Because I always seem to forget.

Forgetting to write,
Writing to remember.

Lost in this combat,
Wanting to remember.

A white knight?
Or
A dark saint?

The pen mightier
Or
The sword?

Each has its day,
But I wonder
If either
Survive the *night*.

Life –
A fleeting memory.

Every important moment,
Every insignificant or hurtful action—
All just fleeting memories
At the very end.

Not able to relive it,
Nothing to remind me.
If I ever get lost,
Would I ever find me?

Would I feel lost forever,
Or just go along with it?
Becoming someone my old self
Would find a stranger.

Someone I'd love,
Or
Someone I'd hate?

Someone I'd *recognize*,
Or
Someone I'd *forget*?

Oh, to write a book,
Of all my greatest sorrows.
A book so dark,
It helps you see the light.
The light in your life.

Like all the greatest sorrows,
Starting off with magic
And ending so *tragic.*

This book that touches them both,
Will touch you—
Within the flesh and bones
You blindly call yourself.

Temporary people be the best.
They display the perfect picture,
And disappear before you see the rest—
The dirty laundry,
The messy cupboards,
Everything behind rose-tinted glasses.

Making the moments we share,
Though meaningless,
Feel so *enchanting*…

While leaving you in a mess.

About the Author

Anaha writes poetry that feels deeply personal and relatable. She is from Bengaluru and has studied Architecture. Her previous work includes her debut poetry collection 'Eclipsed Hues' which follows the emotional journey from childhood to adulthood.

She writes with the intent of helping her readers feel heard, understood and most of all, feel a little less lonely. She writes about heartache, anger, internal conflicts and the small beautiful moments we tend to miss out on. She believes pain can be beautiful too and tries to help her readers see that.

Outside of writing, she enjoys singing, traveling, teaching under- privileged kids or just spending time with her cat and guinea pig.

You can find her at:
https://www.instagram.com/author_anaha

9 789334 342819

Printed at Repro India Ltd.